Everything Is Going to Be Okay
Godly Strategies For The Seasons Of Life

Dee Reeves

© 2019 Warrior Services, LLC
All rights reserved. No portion of this book may be reproduced, photocopied, stored, or transmitted in any form –except by prior approval of the author or the publisher, except as permitted by U.S. copyright law.

Printed by
Warrior Services, LLC
McDonough, GA

Unless otherwise noted, all Scripture quotations are taken from the NEW INTERNATIONAL VERSION of the Bible.
Printed in the United States of America
U.S. Copyright No. Pending: 1-7884126701
ISBN: 978-1-733286008

Table of Contents

Acknowledgments 5
Introduction 7
Chapter 1: The Shattering 13
   Chapter 1 Prayer 18
   Chapter 1 Declaration 19
Chapter 2: Shut the Door 23
   Chapter 2 Prayer 27
   Chapter 2 Declaration 28
Chapter 3: Your Choice 33
   Chapter 3 Prayer 40
   Chapter 3 Declaration 41
Chapter 4: Defensive Stance 45
   Chapter 4 Prayer 49
   Chapter 4 Declaration 50
Chapter 5: The Great Illusionist 55
   Chapter 5 Prayer 60
   Chapter 5 Declaration 61
Chapter 6: Cry Baby, Cry 65
   Chapter 6 Prayer 70
   Chapter 6 Declaration 71
Chapter 7: Close in ranks 75

Chapter 7 Prayer 83
Chapter 7 Declaration 84
Chapter 8: The Struggle Birthed a Warrior 89
Chapter 8 Prayer 92
Chapter 8 Declaration 93
Connect with Me 100

Acknowledgments

All praises to God through all blessings flow. If it had not been for the Lord on my side, where would I be? I praise Him for being the visionary behind this book. I praise Him for the work He will do through the words on these pages of this book and the healing He will bring to many. Father, we have come a long way together, and I know we get through anything together.

To my children, Juwan, Asya, and Amber and my grandbabies, Jayden and Ava for showing me how unconditional love looks and for helping me to realize it's okay to be authentically you! I pray you receive healing and love through this book as well.

To my late parents, Mary and Alfred, thank you for showing how me to live Holy. You taught me how to embrace life. Thank you to my mother for every prayer in the house and every hymn song!

To my siblings, nieces, nephews for the calls, texts, prayers, push, and love. For accepting me for me! Even the tough love. Especially love to my late sisters, Dorothy and Lou Anna, for showing me the strength through your life examples.

To my in-laws for your love and acceptance.

To Yvette and Gerald Benton (G.Y.M.) for interceding for me in prayer when I was barren. For allowing God to use you to breathe new life into this dead woman and for calling me out the fighter in me! I thank you PUSHERS!! To my V.O.V. family, the warriors for pouring into me. Special thanks to Dr. Katrina Foster, the mouth of the body which V.O.V. for speaking it, editing every word, and keeping the work as God intended.

Thank you to every Kingdom connection I have made in my life, especially in this season. You have held me up when I couldn't hold myself. Many blessings to the person reading this book. I pray it blesses you abundantly and you know ...

Finally, thank you to my husband Michael for loving me. I pray that you will see the great things God has for you PPK. Thank you for every forehead kiss!

Everything's going to be okay...

Introduction

There's a strategy to gain and maintain your freedom. The enemy doesn't want you to know this because if you figure it all out, you would be victorious and there would be no way that you would ever feel victimized again. You would wake up from your dead state and become a mighty weapon. There's a strategy that will bring you behind enemy lines and become VICTORIOUS!

As I lay there in my bed, tears rolling down my face and unable to sleep, I was experiencing my regular 3am wake call. I was calling on the Lord just to help me. I prayed and cried and cried and prayed. I couldn't fix this one. "The Fixer" couldn't fix where she was at that moment. As I called on the Lord at my wit's end, the words came out, "Help me Lord." I heard God say, "Everything's going to be okay..." It was almost like someone grabbed my face like a little kid and spoke and a peace came over me. I opened my Bible, and there came the confirmation. Romans 8:28, "And we know that all things work together for good to them that love God, to them who are the called according to his purpose."

As I fell asleep in my tears, I began to dream. Nightmares had become frequent, but this dream was different. I was on an island, vacationing with one of my friends. As we got the beach, our tour guide began to tell us that in order to get to the other island, we had to take a ferry boat. As I turned, I missed the boat. I watched as my friend sail away. I begin to think, "I'm stuck!"

Let me give you a little background about me. I can't swim. Yes, I'm a Navy Veteran, but I can't swim. I hate the boats to the point where I can't even watch the movie Titanic. A boat ride for me is unimaginable, and there I was asking the tour guide about getting on the next boat so I could go to the other island, almost to the point of urgency. That's how I felt in this season, too. I just wanted to get out of this season on to the next island, place, or whatever. As I listened to the tour guide, and I looked at the clear blue water and the distance between the two islands, I heard the tour guide say. "You can swim, it's not far." Then I heard myself say, "I can swim! I can swim?!" And I began to swim in the water without fear or distress.

I woke up out of that dream feeling powerful, with so much hope. As I prepared for my day, I opened up my Bible to the scripture for that day, Isaiah 43:1, "Fear not: for I have redeemed thee, I have called thee by thy name; thou art mine." This made me so excited! Holy Spirit then instructed me to continue reading. And there it as Isaiah 43:2," When thou passest through the waters, I will be with thee; and through the rivers, they shall not overflow thee: when thou walkest through the fire, thou shalt not be burned; neither shall the flame kindle upon thee."

That was it. I knew it at that point. If I was going to make through to the other island and make out of this season, I couldn't do it alone. I had to do while holding the hand of my Father. But I was going to make it, and it was all going to work out for my good. There IS a strategy, and the enemy doesn't want you to know it because if you figured it out, there would be NO way you would ever feel victimized again….

Everything's going to be okay...

Everything's going to be okay

Chapter 1
The Shattering

During any catastrophic event, you always hear guidance after the incident happened. When an earthquake occurs, experts say prepare for aftershocks. When a hurricane happens, experts say don't go outside. Watch out for power lines. You are told to be aware of your surroundings when a tornado hits. They tell you to prepare and go to your basement, but they also say don't move anything. Wait for assistance. It's the same way when you're dealing with life situations, sometimes the most danger happens after the event.

Heartache.

Loss.

Brokenness.

Betrayal.

What about those events that happen where you had no preparation time? Your life is very important, so what do you do? How do you react? In this case, the decisions you make will be the most important after the situation. Even after you've been bumped and bruised, you have to decide what you are going to do after the incident occurs. We want to react immediately, but sometimes no reaction is the best reaction.

As they were growing up, I told my children never to let another person's actions cause you to react because once you do, you have lost all control because you've given your power over to someone else. It may sound like I'm telling you to sit back and become a doormat for someone else, but I'm not. I'm telling you to react in a way that the Father wants you to respond.

Sometimes not moving, not making a decision that other people think you should make, and not reacting in a way that you probably have all cause to react in is really the way you should respond. You have to do what God wants you to do.

Sometimes it's better just to sit and wait. The Bible even says they that wait upon the Lord shall renew their strength. So, when you pause and listen to that still, small voice from God, then you're able to make a better choice for you and your future. We're not always prepared for catastrophic events. Sometimes a wet weather condition comes out of nowhere. It's like hail. One day is beautiful and sunny, and the next second there's a thunderstorm. There's nothing that you can do about it but run for shelter. You can find temporary shelter, but, eventually, you're going to have to come out of that hidden place. But before you come out, you have to make sure that the coast is clear. Make sure that you come out the right way. Make sure that you are really prepared. The aftershock of situations has caused people more depression and anxiety then the actual situation itself. They are consumed with thoughts--How am I going to deal with this?? This was not what I signed up for! This is not how it was supposed to be!! In this case, don't act and have another person's actions control you in the situation. The person in control in any situation is always the person that can see things around them. You're able to see more precise about what's going on after the storm subsides.

In the same way, before you go out and make decisions, I encourage you to take the time to listen to the Father, read, study, pray, fast, and get yourself ready so when you step out into that broken, torn up place, you'll be able to make sound decisions based upon the Word of God.

Chapter 1

Prayer

Father, as I go through this time, I surrender my heart to You. Although I cannot understand the things I am experiencing, I know that You are in full control. Protect and keep me when I am feeling down. I know You are there to lift me. Your purpose for my life is far bigger than I ever imagined. I pray You get the glory out of this time and this experience.

Chapter 1

Declaration

I declare as Your word says that latter shall be greater than my former. I am fearfully and wondrously made in Your image. The purpose and plans of my life are in Your hands, and my steps are ordered by You alone.

My Notes and Strategies

Chapter 2

Shut the Door

One day, I was led by the Holy Spirit to go on a fast. 30 days. No food or water from sunrise to sunset. I never fasted like that before. I cried out to God, saying, "How am I going to do this!?! I need you to give me strategies! I need you to tell me how I'm going to live through all this!" At this point, I had been through the ups and downs and was feeling very disjointed. I had never been in this season before, so I was unsure as to what I was supposed to do next. I was trying to trust God and believe what He was saying in His Word, but I knew I needed some help. So, I decided to go on a fast. I said, "God, give me something every day." I started paying attention more intentionally. My eyes started opening up to things that were around me, and my spiritual vision became so much clearer. Then I started writing different things God gave to me. The first thing He told me to do is spend more time with Him. I naively thought, "But I'd go to church three times out the week—sometimes four. I read my Bible. What are you saying? I spend time with you. I'm doing my best!"

Then, I walk into my daughter's room and knock on the door. She says, "I can't talk right now. Can you give me about an hour? This is the time I spend with God. Here was my twenty-two year-old (at the time) telling me that she can't talk to me because she needs to spend time with God! I was so proud of her, so I started asking her questions about the time she spent with God. She explained that she has a routine every Sunday (whether she goes to church or not) to shut off everything for 1-2 hours to speak to God, read her Bible, and write.

I started to use this strategy as is, but God pushed me to extend myself. He said that He had to be my all—no one else. It had to be just Him and me. I decided to turn my phone off at 10:00 pm so I could spend that time reading the Bible, pray, listen to YouTube videos, or whatever God put on my heart to do during that time. That time was now dedicated to Him, but I told Him if I was going to make it through this, He would have to be there and hold my hand. Then I realized that I would have to hold His hand too and I couldn't let go because we were in this together. I continued to read Romans 12:12 and Hebrews 13:15-16 to keep myself encouraged during this time.

As I continued my fast, I continued to look for the strategies that God has given me to use, and they started to pour! But I know for certain that if I didn't exercise the first strategy I would have never been able to hear God clearly enough for Him to show me the complete process.

I constantly sought the guidance of the Holy Spirit. I would like to make this point certain to you ALL.

There is no way that you will be able to make it with a true connection to the Father and the Holy Spirit abiding in you constantly. You must seek Him in prayer, dropping all the weights of the world and surrendering yourself to Him fully!

Chapter 2

Prayer

Father, You have been there with me in the secret place. You have hidden me in my darkest place. I nestle closely to You and trust Your direction.

Chapter 2

Declaration

I declare that You are the King of my heart and my spirit. You are my all and all. I will follow You from this day forward. I will keep Your commandments and do what Your will for my life.

My Notes and Strategies

Chapter 3
Your Choice

Don't let anyone determine who you are or how you should feel about a situation. 9 times out of 10, they wouldn't know what to do if they were in the same season you are in. In Galatians 3:6-9 (the Message version), the Bible says, answer this question: Does the God who lavishly provides you with His presence, his Holy Spirit, working things in your lives you could never do for yourselves, does he do these things because of your strenuous moral striving or because you trust him to do them in you? Don't these things happen among you just as they happened with Abraham? He believed God, and that act of belief was turned into a life that was right with God. Is it not evident to you that persons who put their trust in Christ (not persons who put their trust in the law!) are like Abraham: children of faith? It was all laid out beforehand in the Scripture that God would set things right with non-Jews by faith. Scripture anticipated this in the promise to Abraham: "All nations will be blessed in you."

So those now who live by faith are blessed along with Abraham, who lived by faith—this is no new doctrine! And that means that anyone who tries to live by his own effort, independent of God, is doomed to failure. Scripture backs this up: "Utterly cursed is every person who fails to carry out every detail written in the Book of the law."
In this season, your faith is being cultivated by the way you see yourself and also the way others see your situation. If you saw yourself today with great faith in your God, you would see and know

that you are fearfully and wondrously made in His image. You would understand that, as His child, certain blessings are automatically due to you. You would know that your Father is in control. Therefore, you would rest easy, knowing that all things will work out for your good. But do you see yourself as the Father sees you? Do you see that your Father can move mountains? He can cause walls to fall. He can change water into wine. Or are you so distracted by looking at everything around you that you don't see who your God is and who you are?

I promise you—the devil would not be after you and you wouldn't have gone through troubles if he didn't already know how powerful you are. It's okay to feel a certain way about being in a situation. But you also have to understand your position in that situation. Are you a victim or are you victorious? Don't allow anyone to determine how you feel. Continuing to stay in Christ and not reacting a certain way does not mean that you are less powerful or that you are weak. You're a strong man or woman of God. You're strong because you're able to stand in this season and you're still living and breathing because you've given all your trust to God. If the people who have given you advice and spoken doom and damnation over your situation were put in your shoes, do you think they would survive, or would they quit? They don't know what they would do! Therefore, you have to protect your ear gates and your eye gates.

There are going to be people naysayers and doubters in your life always. For the rest of your life, you're going to have to deal with people who don't understand you and your God. You'll be given advice on how to handle situations in a certain way. You'll be given advice on how to take revenge. But I must caution you—Vengeance is mine saith the Lord. There is no reason for you to start plotting on how you're going to get revenge. Do you want revenge, or do you want victory? Victory is so much better than revenge. It's never positive when you try to take matters into your own hands. Let the Father have control. I want you to see your power and the power of the Holy Spirit that dwells within you through your faith. I want you to understand that if you trust in the Lord with all your heart and lean not on your own understanding, He shall direct your path. Your path is directed by the Father is surely much better than your path being directed by your friends.

Let me give you a clue into these people who are telling you things that are not lined up with the Word of God. They're bitter. They didn't do what you're doing now. When they were going through a situation, they didn't rely on the guidance of God. They didn't rely on the input of the Father.

They let their emotions take control. Now they live a life that is resentful and bitter.

I know that's not nice, but it's true. Most people give you advice are speaking out of their hurt. They're not giving you information that is going to take you to another level. Once I attended a women's conference and the woman that woman of God who spoke said, "Pray for an individual. Pray for your spouse. Pray for your children. Pray about the problems with your job. Do you want God to do the driving? If you let someone else take the wheel, they will crash and burn crash and burn. Your job is to pray."

Do you remember back in the day when we had those bad advice columns in the newspaper? Someone will write and say, "Suzy I'm going through this issue. I need your advice." All we know is that Suzy would give you some advice. Would you take it? I don't know. But I'd rather give my advice and my information from the

Father. I'd rather wait on him because he knows my future. He knows my ins and outs. He designed every bit of me, so he knows what makes me tick. All He wants is the best for me. So, this is one of my strategies— Don't let anyone determine who you are or how you should feel about the situation you're in. Don't let anyone tell you it's not good to be loving to someone, it's not good to trust, or it could never work out. When those people start talking, you start walking. Trust in the Lord with all your heart and lean not on your own understanding. He will direct your path.

Chapter 3

Prayer

Lord, let the words of my mouth and the meditation of my heart be acceptable unto You. When those around me do not understand me or don't believe as I do, let me follow You. Let me hear no other voice but Yours.

Chapter 3
Declaration

I declare today that my ears, eyes, and mind are covered in the blood of Jesus. All negative words and words that were spoken against the promises of my life are canceled.

My Notes and Strategies

Chapter 4

Defensive Stance

Have you ever been in a battle and you just wanted to plead your case? I used to spend more time pleading my case than getting on my knees. In those situations, I would think: Don't you see the writing on the wall? Don't you see the train wreck that's about to happen? Don't you see the good in me? Don't you see what's right? Don't you see the mistakes that are happening? Don't you see what you're doing? I used to spend more time trying to let other people see that I was on the right instead of just trusting the Father until the Lord helped me to realize that sometimes silence is the best strategy you can employ. Some situations do not require you to say anything or do anything. Your defensive stance in a situation is going to make the difference. Offense sells tickets but defense wins games. How are you going to approach this battle as the enemy comes at you and attacks you from every way? Are you going to be in a position where you're like gangbusters and go on the attack or are you just going to stand still and let the Lord fight your battles? Standing still and letting the Lord fight your battles can seem like the most difficult thing in the beginning of the process when you're going through struggles. However, sometimes the best fight that you can do is fight in silence. The best fight you can give is trusting that the Father has an ultimate outcome that is going to make everything that you've gone through worth it. If there's going to be a battle, the Lord is going to show Himself worthy. In 2 Chronicles 20, we see how the Lord delivered the huge armies of Moab and Ammon into the hands of Jehoshaphat. He spoke through Jahaziel, the son of Zechariah, "Do not be afraid of this huge army, The battle is not yours. It is God's. You will not have to fight this battle."

You too will not have to fight this battle. I know you can't hide. You can't run. You can't take shelter. Eventually, you're going to have to come out and face the situation. So, how are you going to face it? Are you going to face it knowing that the battle was already won? Are you going to face it by reacting by everything that comes around you? Are you going to be disturbed by the bees on a buzzing or other things that are going on around you? Or are you going to trust the Father so much that you're not going to worry about what happens next? In 2 Chronicles 20, they worshipped the Lord. That's what you're going to have to do. Continue to praise God. Find your defensive stance. In this particular scripture, their enemies ended up turning on themselves. They didn't have to do anything. They just praised and worshipped God. I admonish you to trust God and let Him fight, even if you don't know or understand how He's going to do it. Don't argue with a fool. You end up looking like a bigger fool. Stay silent. You will not have to fight this battle. God has already won. Declare victory!

Chapter 4
Prayer

God, even though the battles may be raging my soul is at peace. In Jesus' name, I will stand firm and see the salvation of the Lord. The peace of God is here with me and fighting on my behalf. I will no longer allow my flesh to remove me from my correction position in battle.

Chapter 4
Declaration

I declare that on this day every battle is WON. Every victory is the Lord's. Nothing shall overcome me. I declare that the opposition has been destroyed and the power of God is ALWAYS WINS!

My Notes and Strategies

Chapter 5

The Great Illusionist

To be honest, I was still struggling. I felt like I was swimming in twelve feet of water and running out of breath fast. I didn't know how long and hard a fast was. I was at the midpoint of my fast, and the devil started throwing fiery darts at me through social media. I quickly learned that social media could be your worst enemy. Your eyes can be your worst enemy. The devil will use your eyes and tricks in front of you make you think things that are there that aren't there and vice versa. When you believe something that is not real, your vision will cause you to fail. Don't believe the façade. Illusions are all around you, so don't believe everything you see. We can be anybody on social media. We can make up whatever we want to make ourselves look a certain way. But when those doors are closed, we have to deal with reality. God pointed me to 2 Corinthians 4:4, Matthew 6:1, and Psalms 101:3-24 to keep me grounded against this trick of the enemy. I learned to reaffirm the truth that there will be some victory on the other side of this. I chose to believe my God, not the façade I see with my eyes.

You can't be disturbed by the things around you.
This is why you have to protect your eyes.
This is why you have to protect your environment.
This is why you have to keep your eyes straight ahead.

Proverbs 4:25-27 says,
Let your eyes look straight ahead;

fix your gaze directly before you.

Give careful thought to the paths for your feet and be steadfast in all your ways.
Do not turn to the right or the left; keep your foot from evil."

In this text, God is telling us that we have to keep our focus on Him. We can't worry about the situations that have gone on around us. We can't worry about the decisions that are being made around us by other people. We are directed to keep our eyes, ears, mind, and thoughts on Him by listening to Him and seeking His perfect will for our lives. We can't be disturbed by what the enemy is doing or what is going on around us. We won't be shaken and taken off-balance in what we're doing. Consider this—when a boxer is in a boxing ring, notice he's not worried about the crowd or what's going on around him. His mind is focused on that opponent in front of him. His mind is based on the win. Have you ever seen how champion players like Venus and Serena are on the court during a tennis match? While they're playing their opponent, they're not worried about anything going on around them. All you see and hear are the balls going back and forth. But their mind and thoughts are on getting to the next set.

That's the fixed mindset you have to have. You have to have a big smile of a tennis player...the big smile of a boxer in a boxing ring...keep your eyes on the prize so that you can't be disturbed by the things gone around you or how something may appear. The biggest reason a bully wins is intimidation. A bully makes you think that they are more powerful than you. That's how a bully defeats anyone. That's how the enemy does. He makes you think that the thing that you are going through is bigger than you. It may seem to be bigger thank you, but if you're innocent than know there's nothing greater than your God. The enemy's plans can never be stronger than your God. Keep your mind fixed on Him and not worry about the facades, illusions, struggles you're going through, decisions of other people, or what's going to happen next. If you keep your mind on Him and stay within His will, then you'll be more successful. I promise you will be less stressed. I promise you will have less of all those emotional, out of body experiences that you have been having. Eventually, you have none of them.

Don't worry about the facades.
It's all an illusion.
Don't believe the hype.

Chapter 5

Prayer

Allow me to have spiritual sight to see past the fog and clouds. Whatever the enemy attempts to use in this world to try to break me will not prosper. I will not believe the lies, illusions, or attacks of the enemy.

Chapter 5

Declaration

I declare that the weapons of this warfare are not carnal but mighty for the pulling down of strongholds. These strongholds that have attempted to hold me back are rebuked and removed. I will no longer allow the things before me to shake me. I will trust You God with all the things of this world. My mind is stable, and I am at peace. The torments of the enemy have been broken.

My Notes and Strategies

Chapter 6
Cry Baby, Cry

Some moments you may feel like you are crashing and burning. Some moments your eyes may be filled to the brim with tears. You may think I'm not supposed to have bad days. I'm not supposed to cry. I'm not supposed to feel this way. Yes, you are. It's okay to have bad days. What is not okay is for you to stay in the position of feeling inadequate and broken. We have trouble when we start believing the worst instead of speaking to your God and declaring positive things over yourself. It's okay to have bad days from time to time.

Furthermore, the worst thing you can do is to tell someone who's fallen apart not to cry. It's okay to cry. Let it all out. Otherwise, when you finally explode all those people around you are going to feel your hurt, and they will start giving you advice that they wouldn't keep to themselves.

Your family will feel it, your children, your spouse, even the postman. And then, you will start going through the same cycle again.
It's okay to have a bad day.
I give you permission to cry your eyes out.
I give you permission to go in your shower, close the door, and scream.

Not every day you have is going to be perfect.
But, even though you're having a bad day, it doesn't mean all is lost.

It doesn't mean that God can't get the victory out of your life or out of this situation.

It doesn't mean that's it or ever will be.

In Psalms 119:28 says, "My soul is weary with sorrow; strengthen me according to your word." Let your Father know that you are feeling down. Broken. Hurt. Tell God, "This doesn't feel good. God, I need your strength to make it. I need your strength to get to where I need to go."
I know it's not fair. It's not your fault.

But it's going to be okay, for In Psalms 34:18, the Bible says, "The LORD is close to the brokenhearted and saves those who are crushed in spirit."

One of my favorite people in the Bible is Hannah. She was a woman who was unable to have children. Her husband still loved her, but she cried and wept bitterly about her unfortunate circumstances. In 1 Samuel 1, we read that Hannah poured our aching heart and her desire for a child to God. Even as she went to the temple and pray, it was thought that she was drunk, but she wasn't. She was in distress. She was distraught. She was desperate. In her prayers, she made a promise to God. She said if He gave her a child, she would dedicate this child back to Him. In His perfect timing, God wiped away her tears and gave her the thing she wanted. She wanted a child, and God gave the desires of our heart. So, if you're going to cry, go ahead and cry.

It's okay to have a bad day. I'm sure Hannah had plenty of bad days as she dealt with not being able to bear a child. Even in her depressed state, she continued to seek God and petition Him for help and healing. At this point, I want to give you some healthy advice. After obtaining these strategies, I tapped into the Holy Spirit and realized that I had reached a point where I couldn't keep going with just me. He always brings you a resource. I urge you to go and seek out counseling. Healing and deliverance, along with counseling, is extremely beneficial. Seek a counselor that is Christian led and is filled with the Holy Spirit so that he or she can access things that you may not know and you cannot see. If you have more bad days than good days, please listen to the Father and let Him lead you to where you need to go to get the help you need.

Chapter 6
Prayer

The Lord has counted all of my tears. He has marked each one with a specific blessing for me. My heart is mended! I will allow the Father to do the work within me as I continuously surrender to You.

Chapter 6
Declaration

I declare that today my tears will become like a river, and my blessings will run over with peace and blessings. I will continually lay my heart at Your feet. I declare that I am healed, delivered, and set free in Jesus name.

My Notes and Strategies

Chapter 7
Close in Ranks

Wow. Close in ranks? I'm a social butterfly. I love people. I will speak to a stranger on the street and ask how they're doing. I just love people. I love them, but the Lord was telling me it was time to close in ranks. Not everyone is for you.

"Closing in ranks" is a military term. The military has a practice of closing the space in between them as the troops are being deployed across the battlefield so the enemy will have a harder time separating them. They're moving in closer and closer together, merging to make a more unified format and foundation to attack their enemy.

Webster defines close in ranks as "being united heaven a united front to defend themselves from severe criticism or when a party closes and ranks around a leader to free to defend him." \ I started evaluating the people around me by looking at what they gave to me and what they did not give to me. I need to make sure that I was not hearing from anyone but God. I had to make sure that the people around me were not trying to take me away from what God was showing me. So, I started deleting their numbers out of my phone. Some I hadn't heard from in a while. Some I knew were not going to give me the type of positive feedback and support I needed during this season. Then, I looked at my social media account. I started removing people that I had been friends with for over 20 years. I had to close in ranks NOW. God told me that not everyone should have access to you. I needed to build a team around me. I couldn't just have anyone on my team. Who wants to be on a team that doesn't support one another? Who wants to be on a team that they're not there to pick you up when you're down in the trenches? That's not a team!! I've been on plenty of teams in my life. Starting as a little girl playing sports to adulthood being in the military and various work teams, I learned that for us to be successful as a team, we had to be united for one goal. The goal was to win. Every team wants to win and fight to the end. We don't want one person going in a different direction from the team and giving up or throwing in the towel. We don't want a negative person on our team.

So, I started looking at my team, my inner circle, those I trusted. I took a good look, and it amazed me. Their words weren't even aligned with the vision God intended for my life. Some were controlling and manipulating. Others were using their life experiences to determine my ultimate outcome. The worst thing that you can do is not to have a group of individuals on your team who are not looking for you to win. Your team should be people who are looking for you to WIN and for God to get the victory out of your life. Who do you have on your team? Do you have people on your team or a group of friends that you know they are just waiting for you to react? They wonder: Why haven't you responded like they think you should respond? Why aren't you bitter and broken?

Do you have people on your team that are allowing you to have "out of body experiences" where you react out of emotion? I told the Lord that I was through with having out of body experiences where I was reacting out of your flesh and emotions. Your team has to be your accountability partners. Your team won't allow you to fail. Your team will support your decision as you align with the Father's will for your life. Your team will continuously encourage and motivate you. Your team will know who you are and be accepting of your true identity in Christ.

They won't try to make you be who they think you should be. I have developed a team of people around me that are accepting of who I am. They know that my decisions are based on the Father, and they love me as I am. My team is not trying to change me. When you close in ranks and you look at the people around you, it makes it harder for the enemy to come in and try to take away what it is that God is doing with you. Your team is constantly looking for any misstep in an attempt to make you fail. Your team won't let you react a certain way because your team knows that if you react a certain way, then the whole team falls apart.

I have been on some successful teams. One of those teams was a softball team. We were the Renegades. Everybody knew our team was the team to beat. I was the catcher on the team and one of my best friends, Cassie, was the pitcher. We had a great bond on and off the field. When Cassie was on the mound, and her pitching may be off, I would encourage her. I was saying things like, Come on--we can do this. Look at the glove. Just look at my glove. Don't be shaken. You've got this. You're going to have a whole bunch of team players, but you must remember—but your biggest supporter will be the Father constantly encouraging you through his word to keep pressing, keep moving, keep trusting. The Father is guiding you. He's saying, "You can do this. Just keep your eyes on the prize. Just keep your eyes on the ball. Keep your eyes steadfast. You can do this! We are almost there, one more inning. You can't quit now." Could you imagine if my friend, the pitcher, would have decided in the middle of the game that she didn't want to be the pitcher anymore? I've seen her get frustrated to the point of giving up, But the Coach would come of the dugout and give her stern talk saying, "Quitting is not going to happen!" He wouldn't allow her to give up! The same rules apply to our lives as believers. We can't keep giving up. When struggles and life challenges come, you can't give up! Your team shouldn't allow you to give up! You can do this!" Your team is vital! One example of a great team is the "Fab Five." The Fab Five, the 1991 University of Michigan men's basketball team that is considered by many to be one of the most exceptional recruiting classes of all time.

The members of the Fab Five—Chris Webber, Jimmy King, Ray Jackson, Jalen Rose, and Juwan Howard—weren't just known for winning but playing a team. All of them became great professional basketball players. In college, they were a team that showed their support of the team and close in ranks. They protected the team. Even today, you see Jalen Rose and Juwan Howard continuing this close team relationship as a true team. Just like the Fab Five, your team is critical. Your team is comprised of the people you allow to be in your life. These are the people you grant access to you to speak on you in your life. I'm not telling you that you should be rude and shut people out of your life. But, in your innermost circle, there has to be a standard. There has to be a person or people who will say, "No, you're a woman of

God. You're a man of God. This is not the way we're going to do this. We're going to do this way. We're going to do it the proper way." Having the right team in place ensures that you are going to win in the end because God is going to give the victory. No matter what happens—in the end, the Father WINS!

Chapter 7

Prayer

Most matchless, Father God, I know that I'm not alone. I thank You for allowing me to see that You are my constant source. Allow me to show the love of God to all I encounter. Let me continue to be the child of God that You intend for me to be. Let others see You through me. Allow me to continue to trust You because You make no mistakes.

Chapter 7

Declaration

I declare today that the spirit of abandonment, neglect, and rejection have been canceled. I am healed from all distress, hurt, and brokenness. I will not live in offense and loss. I will be an influencer in the world. I will not be influenced by the things that are not aligned with Your will for my life. I am a VICTOR and not a victim in Jesus name.

My Notes and Strategies

Chapter 8
The Struggle Birthed a Warrior

After my 30 days of fasting was over, I washed my face and said I would never feel that way again. This struggle birthed a Warrior! Then, I started meeting more people who were going to the next level. I started opening my eyes more. I started reading my Bible more. I had taught Bible study for years. I had taught kids about the Word of God. I had even helped with the Bible team. But I never knew the Word for myself. I never knew the power behind my prayers. One day I woke up, and the Holy Spirit told me that I needed a prayer closet. I had watched the movie War Room probably two or three years before but didn't understand what she was doing when she went into the chamber and shut the door. I wanted to be obedient to the Holy Spirit's promptings, so I cleared off everything in my shoe closet, bought myself a little pillow, and started putting my petitions in there. I started speaking to God, telling Him what I wanted and what I needed. Every day I began to go in the closet, call on His name, and tell Him, "Thank you!" If it weren't for Him, I would've lost my mind a long time ago.

If it weren't for Him, my children would be lost. If it weren't for him, my husband would probably be somewhere dead.

I immediately started seeing the greatness that was behind my prayers. I started having people in my life that would tell me your prayers were powerful. I realized that God had given me all those tools and that He was sharpening them up as I was learning, reading, and studying more. I also realized that I didn't need to rely on other people to show me what to do—He was giving me direction. I didn't need to call my friend in a midnight hour when I was crying, broken, and hurt. He was giving me comfort when I was alone and didn't know what to do. He was showing me the strategies to make it through whatever I was going through so that I could be stronger and wiser on the other side. I thank God for all I learned and gained through that 30-day fast. Without question, I knew that I would never be the same again!

So now, YOU, warrior stand up and move. Push beyond the brink. Your purpose and victory awaits you!

Chapter 8
Prayer

Father, thank You for every new thing You have done in me. I thank You for the voice that You have given me. I praise You for opening my mouth and causing walls to fall. I honor Your presence within me. As I continue to birth out the great things You have planted in me, give me wisdom, knowledge, and understanding of Your word. Continue to allow me to be led by Your Holy Spirit and be confident in the work You continue to do within me.

Chapter 8
Declaration

I declare today that I am a mighty warrior. As I grow in the Father, I surrender my will to His will. He will continue to strengthen me. His love is unfailing. I will accept my position in the body of Christ. I declare that I walk without fear.

My Notes and Strategies

_____
_____

"You're a Warrior"

Everything's going to be okay...

My Connections

If you would like to book or schedule events, book signing or connect with me through social media, you may contact me at:

Facebook: @Betty Reeves

Instagram : @onestormyheart

Website: http://deereeves.com

www.ingramcontent.com/pod-product-compliance
Lightning Source LLC
LaVergne TN
LVHW011427080426
835512LV00005B/318